Towards the A
the Natior
European and Na
in Christian Perspective

Richard Franklin

© Sarum College Press 2004

All rights reserved. No part of this publication may be reproduced, stored in a retrieval system, or transmitted in any form or by any means, electronic, mechanical, photocopying, recording or otherwise without prior permission of the publisher.

Published by Sarum College Press in partnership with Ekklesia

ISBN 0 9534836 4 9

Sarum College Press
19 The Close, Salisbury
Wiltshire SP1 2EE
01722 326899
bookshop@sarum.ac.uk
www.sarumcollegebookshop.co.uk

Ekklesia
21 Tooting Bec Gardens
London SW16 1QY
020 8769 8163
office@ekklesia.co.uk
www.ekklesia.co.uk

Sarum College is an ecumenical education, training and conference centre.

Ekklesia is a think-tank that works to promote theological ideas in public life.
It is an initiative of the Anvil Trust, charity no. 1010354.

Cover illustration by Ernesto Lozada-Uzuriaga

SUMMARY

- By and large Christian thinkers have played only a small part in the debate over moves towards political unity in Europe and have paid little attention to its theological significance.

- It is important that Christianity in the EU constitution is not the only issue that Christians focus on.

- The key question is whether we want to preserve national sovereignty? Is this the Christian way? What is the value of national identity? What even is the value of the nation state?

- The spirit of internationalism and universality ('catholicity') that historically has always been at the heart of the Christian faith means that narrow patriotism and nationalistic bigotry are inimical to the gospel.

- Yet in both western and eastern churches Christians have often equated their religion with their national loyalties, and nationalist leaders have used Christianity in its various forms as a tool for the establishment of national cultural homogeneity.

- Seeing one's own nation as specially chosen leads to sinful self-aggrandisement and a failure to recognise that all individuals and communities are subject to universal divine Lordship and judgement.

- The spiritual equality and unity of all Christians and the breaking down of racial, cultural and religious barriers are central to the New Testament and the main currents of Christian political theology.

- The Church must respect the diversity of human cultures while remembering it is not possessed by any particular nation or culture.

- In the judgement of the Protestant theologian Wolfhart

Pannenberg, 'The modern elevation of the nation as the dominant model of political action can be seen as a contradiction to the international traditions of Christianity and to their source in the Christian hope that all humans may participate in the Kingdom of God.'

- Since internationalism is at the heart of Christian political thought it is legitimate to consider whether the nation-state or, indeed, anything short of some kind of comprehensive international political unity can be justified.

- Nation-states must not view themselves as 'ends in themselves'. They are a phenomenon of political history and have had some merits but many defects. In Christian perspective they can have practical, but only transient, value as a step on the road towards the wider political unit implied by the gospel.

- On the question of the best way to accomplish a more internationalist state of affairs, the answer is to proceed step by step. It is impossible to rush or impose an international order and to try to do so will result in disaster.

- The 'Fortress Europe' mentality results from a perception of European unity as based wholly on economic self-interest and is a temptation towards an excluding Empire that must be resisted.

- It is meaningful to speak of an emerging common European culture, which is evident at both elitist and popular levels, but the corresponding European identity must not run counter to national or regional identity.

- Politically the EU exists to allow the flourishing of national, regional and all other forms of collective identity contained within a framework which does not allow our natural differences to develop into anything that is destructive – a Europe in which people can feel comfortable in their many forms of collective identity without having to assert them in such a way as to diminish others.

- Enlargement to 25 members can surely only be welcomed by Christians as bringing more opportunities for close contacts with people from different but complementary cultures.
- In history peace has usually been maintained by the force of arms.
- The peace, justice, democracy and rights enjoyed by the citizens of Europe are upheld by consensual politics. Given Europe's sad history, it can be argued that if the price for this is the inducement of prosperity – one of the attractions for new members - surely it is a price worth paying.
- A main opportunity in forthcoming decades will be to welcome to EU membership countries to the east of the Union's new border, whose culture has been formed by Orthodox Christianity. Can we enlarge our vision to handle what lies ahead in twenty-first century Europe?

FOREWORD

In Europe the twentieth century had two extremely different halves. The first was the bloodiest few decades in the world's history. The second was, in Western Europe, perhaps the most peaceful period in its history. The last decade brought an end to the Cold War but also, in former-Yugoslavia, a terrible resurgence of the militant nationalism that had fomented the world wars.

The question of our national and European identities remains urgent and disputed in the new century. This booklet publishes a lecture given on 1 May 2004, the day of Enlargement of the European Union from 15 to 25 member-states. Richard Franklin addresses that question with a carefulness that the European historical context demands but is absent in a great deal of public comment on it.

At the time of publication, the draft European Constitution is subject to debate. One striking feature of the document is the extensive and impressive treatment precisely of the relations of national and EU-wide institutions.[1] In the Constitution's provisions on this, the principle of subsidiarity is of primary importance. This principle was first articulated explicitly within Christian social thought, in the Papal Encyclical *Quadragesimo Anno* of 1931, written in part to oppose emergent totalitarianism. The churches' record in contributing to the great challenges Europe faced in the twentieth century was a very mixed one, but the influence of Christian political thought in Europe remains great. In the new century, during which growing religious diversity will perhaps displace national diversity as Europe's greatest practical challenge, Richard Franklin's lecture is a contribution with the seriousness and breadth of vision we require.
The lecture was given at a conference of students of Sarum College's Politics and Theology Programme. This offers a wide

range of opportunities for education to equip Christians for public life. Students come from across Britain and from other EU countries. See www.sarum.ac.uk/society

Nicholas Townsend
Director, Politics and
Theology Programme
Sarum College

Jonathan Bartley
Director,
Ekklesia

Richard Franklin is the European Officer for the Church of England Diocese of Salisbury. He serves on the Board of Church and Society and regularly publishes Issues Facing Church and Society leaflets for the Diocese. Formerly he was a lecturer in Ethics at Chichester Theological College. He was a founding member of the Society for the Study of Christian Ethics (www.dur.ac.uk/ssce/) and the founding editor of the journal Studies in Christian Ethics in 1987. He has undertaken research on the relationship between the churches and the European institutions, including a period of study spent in Strasbourg.

---

[1] The text can be accessed at http://european-convention.eu.int/docs/ Treaty/ cv00850.en03.pdf (May 2004). See Article 9 and especially the Protocols on 'Application of the Principles of Subsidiarity and Proportionality' and 'The Role of National Parliaments in the European Union'.

Towards the Abolition of the Nation State?
European and National Identity in Christian Perspective

Introduction

The phenomenon of European integration was one of the most striking features of the political history of the second half of the twentieth century. It led to the emergence of major political institutions, above all the European Union. It is a cause of widespread debate and continues to be controversial in some quarters. Early in the twenty-first century two major developments continue to keep the EU at the forefront of the political agenda. The first of these is the much spoken of and written about European Union Constitution. The second is the enlargement of the EU, the addition of ten new member states which occurred on 1st May 2004. By and large Christian thinkers have played only a small part in the debate over moves towards political unity in Europe and have paid little attention to its theological significance. Some major theologians, such as Wolfhart Pannenberg, are exceptions to this general rule, but it is surely high time that a number of leading Christian thinkers attended to this issue. The discussion as to whether or not God and/or Christianity should have a place in the proposed constitution is one issue that Christians – even the Pope – have seriously engaged with in recent years. It is an interesting, even a tantalising issue, and there is more at stake than is at first obvious. It is not so much the matter of whether or not the word God be mentioned, but whether a particular religion be alluded to and in what terms. The inclusivity of the EU is at stake here. Though there are some ardent europhiles who see the European Union as Christendom revivitus, few people believe that one particular religion should be given pride of place in the institution. Reference to the rich inheritance of faith stemming above all from all the Abrahamic religions might well have a place in the constitution and this could be given serious consideration. At the end of the day, however, it is important that this is not the only issue in the constitution that Christians focus on. Otherwise the public perception that the Church is concerned only with the spiritual realm will be reinforced.

In this country at least the bearing of the proposed constitution on national sovereignty is at the forefront of the debate. What do Christians say about that, if anything? It is claimed that the constitution will enshrine and extend the rights of Brussels such that they will encroach upon national sovereignty. The areas under debate include taxation, foreign policy, defence, criminal justice, legal base, social security and asylum. Politicians who wish to defend themselves against partially informed media-led public opinion simply respond that the argument that the new constitution will undermine national sovereignty is a slur, a misrepresentation of realities. They also argue that the constitution is particularly necessary to update the EU as it evolves yet again with ten new members joining and even more in the wings. Whether that is strictly speaking dependent upon accepting the new constitution I question. Surely a curtailment of the power of the veto and increased qualified majority voting is being and can be brought in by other means? But I want to pose a more fundamental question than any of those usually considered by the politicians. It is this: do we want to preserve national sovereignty in any case? Is this the Christian way? And underlying that issue are some even more basic ones. What is the value of national identity? What even is the value of the nation state? And what of European identity? Is there such a thing? How has it been and might it be developed? In order to consider these complex questions I want to begin by looking in detail at the concept of national identity from a Christian theological perspective.

1. A theological evaluation of national identity

National identity is one of the most significant of all forms of bonding. In sociological theory it is generally placed into the category of a natural as opposed to a conventional form of bonding. This distinction, natural – conventional, has some interesting implications in discussions of the merits of the European Union. Some commentators have argued that the EU is flawed because it is an artificial construct rather than a natural entity. I believe this way of thinking owes much to a particularly British style of philosophy. A very important area of disagreement among philosophers lies in the field of perception. Simply put the issue is this: is knowledge gained primarily through sense perception or is it more reliably obtained via self-evident principles? Generally speaking one can say that the British empiricists held the first opinion, the continental rationalists the second. This debate bears on our topic because if your theoretical standpoint is more empiricist, you will tend to give greater weight to communities which appear natural; if you approach things from a rationalist angle you will tend to think that rather more communities are conventional. Those with an empiricist outlook on society will tend to be more sceptical of political 'constructs' because they do not appear natural. Those of a more rationalist inclination will not be so anxious, seeing most societies as constructed though convention. This has important and interesting consequences in attitudes taken towards the formation of international bodies such as the European Union. Those of a more empiricist outlook tend to be rather sceptical about the enterprise, seeing it as 'un-natural', those of a more rationalist turn of mind regard it, along with most other political organisations, as legitimate if it can be rationally defended. It is fascinating to find that a similar observation was made by Harold Macmillan speaking about European unity at the Council of Europe in 1950. "The continental tradition," he said, "seeks to reason *a priori* and descends, as it were from the summit to the plain; it proceeds from general principles, which it then applies to practical issues

... the British, on the other hand, prefer to discuss problems *a posteriori*, ascending from practical experience towards the summit."[1] I once discussed this matter in Strasbourg with an Alsacian Church leader. He simply pointed to the map of Europe he had on his wall and indicated the difference between the clear-cut boundaries of Britain, our coastline, and the ever-changing boundaries of the continental European nations.

But how should the nation and nationalism be assessed? There are many positive things that can be said about the nation. A nation draws together a group of people who have some form of common life probably based, originally at least, in kinship and/or language, sometimes religion. The nation provides a large enough arena in which a common culture can emerge and flourish. A nation gives a people a sense of common history and purpose. People have a sense of participation in determining the fate and destiny of their own nation. In Europe the emergence of nationalism began towards the end of the middle ages and that of the nation state in the late sixteenth and seventeenth centuries but gained its greatest momentum during the nineteenth century. Even before this, however, there had been an increasing tendency to associate the state with peoples with some degree of natural cohesion. In political theory this was linked to the search for legitimacy deriving from the will and interests of those peoples. Alongside ideological developments went economic and technological advances which increasingly led people to identify with their nation rather than just their locality. The spread of vernacular education also played an important part in increasing the sense of national identity.

The Christian evaluation of the nation begins with the Bible where one strand, at least, within the Pentateuch sees the origin of the nations in natural kinship, divinely sanctioned. (See, for example, Deuteronomy 32.8ff. where Yahweh is depicted as giving the nations "their inheritance".) Clearly also the people of Israel play a vital role in the Biblical narrative as the elect nation serving God's purposes. They have entered into a unique covenant with Yahweh who sustains them as a nation. In the Old Testament other nations were always seen in relation to the people of Israel and subservient to their needs and destiny. Another important Biblical tradition, however, understands the origin of different nations as the product of human sin and division. In Genesis 10 and especially Genesis 11 in the story of the Tower of Babel, the human race is divided into separate nations as a result of sin. The New Testament presents us with a vision of the Kingdom of God which relativises all earthly realms, states or nations. The appearance of the Kingdom in the person of Jesus brings the fulfilment of God's calling of the nation of Israel in the opening up of God's elect people to all. In the Church, racial, national and class barriers are cast down (Gal. 3.28). God's ultimate purpose is to draw all nations together in a new heaven and new earth (Revelation 5.9).

In Christian tradition the central strand has always been internationalist. From its inception the Church was international, universal or 'catholic'. The term catholic to describe the Church grew in importance from its earliest found use in the writing of Ignatius of Antioch. Part of the meaning of the concept has to do with the universality of the Church, that it knows no human boundaries. The early Church grew up, however, largely within the Roman Empire whose boundaries were so large as to encompass much of the known world. Although many early Christians were understandably very suspicious of the Empire as from time to time it persecuted them, others saw divine providence at work in the *Pax Romana*. Origen, for example, saw the establishment of the Empire of Augustus as a divine act with the purpose of reducing the difficulty of proclaiming of the gospel. He also maintains that national distinctions will disappear at the coming of the Kingdom of God.[2] Similar ideas can be found in the writings of Melito, Hippolytus and Eusebius of Caesaria, who traces his theology of history back to Luke 2.1ff. where the birth of Jesus is linked to the policies of Caesar Augustus. Eusebius was, of course, writing at the time of the Constantinian conversion of the Empire. After the Roman Empire became Christianised the distinction between earthly and heavenly citizenship became blurred. This led to a tendency, which has long remained in Orthodox and to some extent in Catholic thought, to believe that the prophecy of Revelation that 'The kingdom of the world has become the kingdom of our Lord and of his Christ' (11.15) had been fulfilled and that, therefore, the Roman Empire was effectively a Christian kingdom.

This idea ran into a major crisis within a century as the Roman Empire itself began to crumble. In response, St Augustine of Hippo tried to help Christians to cope with the collapse of the Empire. In *The City of God* he held that no particular human social structure may be equated with God's city and that a Christian's final loyalty is to that city alone. At the same time his view that the heavenly city must transform the earthly was one factor leading to the establishment of the typical medieval view that God had foreordained the given structures of society. His theory of the legitimacy of the earthly city's role in maintaining temporal peace also led, during the middle ages, to the development of the idea of the 'two powers', the secular and the spiritual. The Church continued as the sole universal institution of Christendom using the various states to uphold peace and justice. But neither Augustine nor, indeed, most medieval thinkers, thought of the state in terms of a nation, but as a part of a wider Christian community held together, of course, by the Church. Dante, in *De Monarchia*, went so far as to advocate a world state governed by an international authority. Most theologians, however, spoke of Christendom in terms of a society of independent political societies, the Catholic Church being the uniting force.

In many ways it could be argued that the break up of this Christendom approach precipitated by the Reformation in the west and the fall of the Byzantine Empire in the east led to the development of nationalism. The state was more and more understood to be comprised of groups of people with a common identity, perhaps a single race or language. Underpinning the elevation of the nation was a theology of election. Nations came to understand themselves as called or elect. In the fourteenth century the French jurist Pierre Dubois said that the French people were specially chosen by God and that their King is the leading prince of Christendom. The Spanish saw themselves in a similar way with the 'Catholic Monarch' at their head. In England the conviction that we were an elect nation was very strong in the seventeenth century. It was the belief of men like Cromwell and Milton that God had entered into a solemn covenant with this nation. This idea spread to America and the conviction that the American 'nation' had a 'manifest destiny' owes much to this line of thought, though it also drew upon the frontier mentality which had its roots in the Spanish reconquest of the Moorish territories. In a partially secularised form can we doubt that it continues even to this day?! While these developments were occurring in the west, in the east similar patterns were emerging. After the fall of Constantinople Moscow came to style itself as the 'third Rome' and the Russian nation came to believe it was called by God to be a bastion of the true Orthodox faith. Holy Mother Russia had arrived. And, to take another example, in nineteenth century German Protestant theology, the people or the *volk* were regarded as a divine 'ordinance of creation'.

In the past one hundred years Christian thinkers have analysed these developments. At the forefront has been Roman Catholic social teaching which, in a series of encyclicals from the papacy of Leo XIII onwards, has stressed the legitimacy of a measure of national pride while underlining the importance of Christian internationalism and the danger of misguided patriotism. The Second Vatican Council's document *Gaudium et Spes* sums up this teaching in the following passage:

> Citizens should cultivate a generous and loyal spirit of patriotism but without narrow-mindedness so that they will always keep in mind the welfare of the whole human family

which is formed into one by the various kinds of links between races, peoples and nations.³

The appropriate Christian outlook, according to Vatican II and the whole of this tradition, is a balance between an appropriate patriotism and an appropriate universalism. The Church must respect the diversity of human cultures while remembering it is not possessed by any particular nation or culture. In terms of the Christians' involvement in political life, this tradition emphasises the notion of serving and seeking the common good which is to be pursued at the international as well as the national level: "The universal common good needs to be intelligently pursued and more effectively achieved."⁴

Similar ideas can be found in much modern Protestant and ecumenical ethics, above all in the work of writers whose ideas were influenced by the horrors of the nationalism of the Second World War. The eminent German Protestant theologian Wolfhart Pannenberg, who was conscripted to fight in the *Vermacht* in the last desperate days of the Third Reich, is typical of this approach. He maintains that,

> The modern elevation of the nation as the dominant model of political action is in clear contradiction to the international traditions of Christianity and to their source in the Christian hope that all humans may participate in the Kingdom of God. This is especially obvious in the way that nationalism used biblical ideas to deify the nation and its people. Thus the concept of a chosen people was applied to modern nations such as England or Germany in order to provide them with the prestige of a religious mission.⁵

While allowing for the nation state as a stage on the path towards larger human communities, such as a united Europe, Pannenberg has a broadly negative interpretation of the nation and certainly regards nationalism as an evil. In a similar vein, the

Third Assembly of the World Council of Churches at New Delhi in 1961 saw the emergence of the post-colonial nations as a mixed blessing. On the one hand the new nationalism was seen to be important in overcoming older tribalism, while on the other hand the Church leaders saw the danger of "its possible perversion into policies of antagonism and exclusiveness against other nations."[6] These ideas are surely at one with the bulk of Christian tradition. For there is no doubt the spirit of universalism, internationalism and catholicism which is at the heart of the Christian faith means that narrow patriotism and nationalistic bigotry are inimical to the gospel. It must, of course, be acknowledged that Christians have often equated their religion with their national loyalties and that nationalist leaders have used Christianity in its various forms as a tool for the establishment of national cultural homogeneity. As we have seen, various theological justifications have been given for this, above all that the nation has been chosen by God, probably for some particular purpose and/or that a solemn covenant exists between this particular people and the deity. Among some Christians this continues to be a reason for rejecting the internationalism of institutions like the European Union. However, although there is nothing wrong with a sense that a particular nation has a task under God, the problem with this whole line of thought is that of pride. Seeing one's own nation as specially chosen leads to sinful self-aggrandisement and a failure to recognise that all individuals and communities are subject to universal divine Lordship and judgement. Above all, however, it fails to remember that the spiritual equality and unity of all Christians and the breaking down of racial, cultural and religious barriers are central to the New Testament and the main currents of Christian political theology.

Since internationalism is at the heart of Christian political thought, it is legitimate to consider whether the nation-state or, indeed, anything short of some kind of comprehensive international political unity can be justified. Three points can be made: (i) In Christian political theology the realities of the flawed structures of the human social order have to be taken into account. Although we might ideally desire that there be a peaceful and just world government and, indeed, believe that this is the hope that the vision of the Kingdom of God sets before us, it is impractical to believe that such a state of affairs will be rapidly achieved and, indeed, in the meantime there is need for a stable political order. The point is to make this as good as it can be in an imperfect world. (ii) The second point concerns the nation-state itself. Such states must not view themselves as 'ends in themselves'. They are merely a phenomenon of political history which have had some merit, though many defects. If they are seen, in Christian perspective, as a step on the road towards the wider political unit implied by the gospel, they have some transient value. (iii) The final question that arises concerns the best way to accomplish a more internationalist state of affairs. The answer, surely, is that one has to proceed step by step. It is impossible to rush or impose an international order upon people and to try to do so will only result in disaster. There must be consent (a point to which we shall return later in this paper). At the same time politicians must also show courage and leadership. They must explain, encourage and persuade. Once again Pannenberg has something enlightening to say:

> Harmony among the nations does not come about of itself, as our experience has shown. Therefore international federations will be most successful if they begin with limited groupings, based on a common history and culture, as well as common political and economic interests. In our own time the progress of European integration is an outstanding example of such confederations.[7]

The views of Pannenberg on internationalism may be compared to those of the Church of England's leading moral theologian of our day, Oliver O'Donovan. O'Donovan rejects the notion of world-government as essentially xenophobic and imperialist. He believes that it is important that that there are distinct communities of peoples – nations – and that the eschatological vision of peace is that we should dwell in harmony specifically with those whose homes and communities are different to our own. He even relates this to the Christian understanding of the Shema: "Xenophilia is commanded us: the neighbour whom we are to love is the foreigner whom we encounter on the road."[8] My own judgement is that O'Donovan's views are a little idealistic this side of the eschaton, and that for most people it is the very foreignness of the foreigner that needs to be diminished in order to build a peaceful world. On the other hand it is certainly true that if the EU is an homogenising empire in O'Donovan's sense it would be xenophobic and syncretising of legitimate cultural divergence. His comments would then apply to it with great force. When it tends in that direction, Christians should be critical of it. Rather it is or should be what he calls for, a meeting place of distinct communities in which differences are celebrated but are not the cause of conflict.

The Biblical denunciation of Empires can be levelled against the European project if it is not seen as part of a wider movement - the development of international groupings of interdependent nations. It should also be seen as part of a wider process of building a worldwide community. If we see things in this way the danger that is sometimes called 'Fortress Europe'- seeing Europe solely in terms of a powerful and rich economic union which keeps those inside wealthy while those outside remain impoverished - is reduced. The European construction should be exemplary and ultimately contributing to an international peaceable human order. The 'Fortress Europe' mentality is a temptation towards an excluding Empire that must be resisted. In some ways it arose inevitably as a result of the emphasis placed upon economics in the European construction. European unity based wholly upon economic self-interest will lead to the Fortress Europe mentality - and to reluctant Europeans. If Europe is to integrate then other foundations, political, cultural, moral and spiritual must be laid alongside the economic. The point is clearly made by Keith Archer:

[I]dentity and culture have scarcely figured in the European treaties. At the beginning Jean Monnet stressed the economy, because he saw economic collapse as a cause of World War II and was suspicious of the role of the French political class in the lead-up to it. Since then all treaties have been mainly technical; only Maastricht brought in culture at all. But a European ethos cannot be built by the market alone - particularly now that it is globalized. Monnet himself is said (apocraphally) to have said: *If we were to start again we would start with culture.*[9]

2. An historical evaluation of nationalism

Alongside this theological critique of the nation could be placed an historical critique. Many see nationalism as one of the greatest evils of the modern world, the cause of wars, turmoil and violence across the globe. The last one hundred and fifty years in particular have seen countless conflicts in all parts of the world whose origins may be traced to nationalistic attitudes. The historian Michael Howard asserts that this was true from the beginning of modern nationalism and, indeed, was integral to its development:

> From the very beginning the principle of nationalism was almost indissolubly linked, both in theory and practice, with the idea of war. For ... those Prussian thinkers whose ideas were to be archetypal for so much nineteenth century nationalism, war was the necessary dialectic in the evolution of nations. ... The terrible thing is that, historically speaking, these thinkers were right. It is hard to think of any nation state ... that came into existence before the middle of the twentieth century which was not created, and had its boundaries defined, by wars, by internal violence, or by a combination of the two.[10]

Similarly many of the prejudices and stereotypes of modern life are rooted in nationalism. If today in Britain we regard nationalism as a rather benign force we should not forget the extremely destructive effects it has had and continues to have. The horrors of Northern Ireland, the former Yugoslavia and USSR and central Africa are all evidence of this insidious poison in our own day. The appalling jingoism in the British tabloid newspapers with their attacks on the Germans and French is another example. Such attitudes have a direct effect on individuals causing widespread pain and anguish.

Many in Europe claim there is a resurgence of the 'local' and the 'regional' and that people increasingly find their identity at this level. In some respects this seems to be born out by the facts and there appears to be an increasing movement towards regionalism in the EU at present. At the same time there are also other types of collective identity apart from the national, local or regional which are growing in importance. Social, professional and recreational allegiances are increasingly significant alongside other means of collective identification. Those linked by their use of the internet is one such example in contemporary society. Some post-modernist theorists argue that the nation-state as the primary focus of collective identity is largely obsolete and that people are seeking community in a wide variety of different 'tribes'. These are formed "as concepts rather than integrated social bodies - by the multitude of individual acts of self-identification."[11] However, while it is true that there are many and varied ways in which people are seeking group identity, it is surely premature to speak of the demise of nationalism when in Europe and in other parts of the world many new nations are appearing and secessionist wars abound.

3. A European Collective Identity?

If there are national, regional, local and other forms of collective identity, can it be said that there is any form of European identity? Many thinkers acknowledge the difficulty of characterising 'Europeanness'. It is often characterised with reference to European political values, such as democracy, the rule of law, pluralism etc.. Whether such elements are sufficient to establish a European collective identity is, however, highly questionable. Some thinkers argue (Philip Schlesinger and Anthony D. Smith, for example) that it is also important to highlight the common cultural identity that exists among Europeans. Smith, for example, maintains that

> the heritage of Roman law, Judeo-Christian ethics, Renaissance humanism and individualism, Enlightenment rationalism and science, artistic classicism and romanticism, and above all, traditions of civil rights and democracy ... have created a common European cultural heritage and formed a unique culture area straddling national boundaries and interrelating ... different national cultures through common motifs and traditions.[12]

Among these cultural highlights it is interesting to note that Smith includes Judeo-Christian ethics. As I have argued in relation to the constitution a Christian or a member of any religious community would want to broaden this to include the entire contribution of the spiritual realm to the culture in which we live. Christianity, Judaism, Islam and other religions clearly have an important place in the common European culture and their contribution should not be overlooked. It was partly to ensure that the European project did not forget the spiritual dimension that Jacques Delors began to speak of the importance of discovering a 'soul for Europe'. What he meant by this has been widely debated. In the following simple statement he seems to clarify the matter admirably:

> We are at the crossroads of European history, where the debate about meaning has become a major consideration. The building of Europe is not just an economic and political exercise but also has a spiritual and ethical dimension.[13]

An important issue that arises in relation to the idea of a common European culture is the extent to which it can be fostered. Smith astutely observes that, although there is a need to encourage the appreciation of this collective culture, too much social engineering will be counter productive. Another commentator, Mark Leonard, remarks that the effort so far undertaken to construct a sense of European identity based on "the narrative of cultural highlights and political identity has failed to grab popular imagination."[14] He also asserts that the "cultural narrative is not only abstract but élitist as well. It offers a heritage that is recognisable only to a tiny class of intellectuals and is largely meaningless to the majority of Europeans."[15] Finally he writes, "Even more worryingly, European leaders have often seen European identity in conflict with national identity, which runs counter to most Europeans' aspirations."[16] I believe Leonard makes some interesting points. I tend to think he overstates his argument against the idea of European collective identity based on our common culture but he is surely correct in his view that European identity must not run counter to national, and, we might add, regional, identity.

Leonard in his paper searches for areas in which a sense of European identity may be based. In fact, having rejected one set of cultural bases, he replaces them with another set, based more in popular culture. European holiday-making, European cuisine, European business, youth exchanges, European sport - particularly football - are all sources of a gently emerging popular European culture. A major difficulty lies in the sphere of language, of course, which continues to create barriers and to focus the attention of some Europeans, notably those from the British Isles, elsewhere. But, however much it is resisted, the emergence of English as a *lingua franca* across Europe goes some way to breaking down barriers. An area of increasing importance is the media. In this the work of Schlesinger, to whom I have already referred, is interesting and important. He believes that it is essential to build a common European public space and that the role of the media in this is of vital importance.[17] At the time of accession of the ten new members of the EU, it is also important to consider the enrichment these nations will bring. Countries like Poland, the Czech Republic and Hungary have made an enormous contribution to European culture in history and will no doubt continue to do so. The enlargement can surely only be welcomed by Christians who will have more opportunities to have closer contacts with people from different, but complementary cultures. As O'Donovan might put it, we have more chance for xenophilia! Alongside the enlargement of cultural vision that the new members will bring, there will also be an appropriate challenge to some of the economic and political institutions of the EU. In particular many of us hope that the expansion will bring about an "overhaul [of the] Common Agricultural Policy so that it is better for farmers, consumers, the environment and the developing world" (the words are those of Tony Blair writing in the *Times* of 30th April 2004, p.24). There is indeed much that needs to be reformed in the European Union, but little is achieved by constant sniping, what is needed is for people to become involved and committed and to work for change from the 'heart of Europe' not its periphery.

However important it is to try to establish a sense of a common culture, the political, one might even say the moral, purpose of the European project should not be lost sight of in seeking out a collective identity. Behind the establishment of the various forms of European economic community leading up to the establishment of the EU was the political vision of a Europe in which national differences were no longer the grounds for armed conflict. The founding fathers of the movement towards 'ever greater union', men such as Jean Monnet, who was inspired by a Christian moral outlook, saw the maintenance of peace as the goal. This is spelt out in the Schumann declaration: "Europe will not be made all at once, or according to a single plan. ... the coming together of the nations of Europe requires the elimination of the age-old opposition of France and Germany.....".[18]

Similarly the Treaty of Paris which set up the European Coal and Steel Community speaks of "the contribution an organised and vital Europe can make ... to the maintenance of peaceful relations ... [creating] the basis for a broader and deeper community among peoples long divided by bloody conflicts."[19]

This, surely, continues to give the European project its *raison d'être*. Politically the EU exists to allow the flourishing of national, regional and all other forms of collective identity contained within a framework which does not allow our natural differences to develop into anything that is destructive. Ironically, of course, it is not understood or perhaps not clearly communicated that the enhancement of national and other forms of collective identity within the framework of the safety net of Europe is precisely what the right kind of federalism is all about. It is possible to envisage a form of national life which is not exclusive and founded on an identity over against 'the other' but is inclusive and welcoming of others whilst esteeming one's own national characteristics. This is surely the type of national collective identity which a Christian would want to welcome. It is what the European Union should surely be promoting - a pluralist Europe in which people can feel comfortable in their many forms of collective identity without having to assert them in such a way as to diminish others. It is usually correctly perceived that it is when one's own sense of identity is weak or problematic that one becomes particularly aggressive in asserting it against others. Thus the EU should work to enhance a strong and positive sense of collective identity in its nations and regions and amongst its peoples with their many and varied forms of identity. This is also, it must be added, and perhaps even more so, the task of national governments and those who shape and form public opinion, especially the popular media. Those forms of collective identity which demonise people who are not like us should surely be vigorously discouraged.

4. Enlarging the Vision

It is often maintained, particularly in this country, that the original purposes behind the establishment of the EU have long been transcended. It is said, for example, that conflict between western European nations is now unthinkable. I am not so sure. Indeed, the peace that we enjoy on this continent is in large measure due to the existence of the EU and without it who is to say what would happen? However, it is of course true that there are other reasons for the existence of the Union. In Britain these are always understood as primarily economic. Britain entered the EEC in the 1970s calling it the 'Common Market' and our approach to Europe has always been to see it in terms of its financial benefits. Although other countries have valued its economic advantages, these have not been as paramount to them as they have been to us. For example when the southern, former dictatorships, Spain, Portugal and Greece entered in the 1980s, a large part of the reason for their membership was to embed and enshrine their new and fledgling democratic systems.

This is true also for the countries joining on 1st May 2004. They desire to strengthen their recently established democratic systems, they want to ensure that human rights, so long neglected, are maintained, they want to belong to a family of peaceable nations who have no reason to be at odds with each other. The European Union has successfully shown that this is best accomplished by a flourishing economic partnership, by so tying national economies together that there is no reason or need for enmity between nations. Indeed such enmity would be counter-productive.

It could be argued, of course, that the EU vision panders to the worst side of human nature, because its unity is based on economic foundations, rather than on neighbour love. In other words we are obliged to be good Europeans and live together in peace and harmony because our economies are so closely intertwined that to do otherwise would result in ruin. Pro-European politicians use this as a kind of bribe, arguing that if we leave the EU or become semi-detached we will all become much poorer. Thus there is nothing altruistic or indeed essentially Christian about the institution. At one level this accusation is well founded. Indeed Andrew Goddard in his Grove Booklet, The European Union: A Christian Perspective, sees the idolatry of money as one of the main failings of the European project.2 0 There is no doubt that a Christian must hold up to divine judgement the contemporary obsession with financial gain and consumerism. This applies as much to the EU as it does to other areas of life in which money rules.

On the other hand, it should not be forgotten that those who began the process towards European integration and many of those who maintain it do have a bigger, indeed a more moral vision. This was, and I believe it remains, the maintenance of peace with justice, democracy and human rights throughout the continent of Europe. In history peace has often, perhaps usually, been maintained by the force of arms. The *Pax Romana*, indeed the so-called *Pax Brittanica*, spring quickly to mind. And the 'peace' of the cold war era was also clearly dependent upon the possession of arms, weapons of mass destruction. But the peace, justice, democracy and rights enjoyed by the citizens of Europe is upheld by consensual politics. If the price for this is the inducement of prosperity, then surely it is a price well worth paying. For Christian theology has a realistic not an idealistic estimate of human nature. It accepts that we are indeed flawed and fallible and that systems of government and community based entirely on altruism are unlikely to survive against the pressures of sin and will therefore fast become corrupt. The sad history of twentieth century communism bears witness to this.
There are then three choices: discord and disunity leading potentially to conflict, co-operation based on the principle of the stick (the peace based on arms model mentioned above) or co-operation based on the carrot. European integration in the last fifty years has been based on the last and in the main one cannot

doubt that it has been phenomenally successful. The success of the European project has depended on it being consensual. Not being imposed by force of arms, but by the free willingness of nations and peoples to work together has been fundamental. For this reason I don't think those who believe in the European project should oppose the proposed referendum on the EU constitution, though many would argue against referendums on principle and would maintain that these decisions are better made through 'normal' politics, i.e. at General Elections. There is a view that referendums simply take issues out of mainstream politics. Whatever the case, it is vitally important that on Europe our politicians give strong leadership and clear information, something I would judge this present government has failed to do.

It is, of course, because of the success of the European Union that countries want to join. Why otherwise would there be a queue? From Estonia in the north to Cyprus and Malta in the south, 1st May 2004 saw the accession of countries rich in European history and culture which will carry the European project to its next stage of development. As I have already indicated we cannot doubt that an important motive in their joining stems from these nations' desire to enjoy the economic prosperity of other countries presently in the EU. In addition there are other reasons for countries wishing to join, some of which have already been mentioned. Eight of the ten countries acceding to the Union in this wave were for many years within the Soviet block and the three Baltic states were, of course part of the USSR. The accession of these countries is a particular cause for rejoicing as it represents another important stage in the healing of the wounds of Europe left over from the Cold War, even, we might say from the First and Second World Wars. It is important to remember, of course, that many significant European nations remain outside the European Union, at least for the time being, above all the great European nation of Russia.

At least three areas of difficulty could face the European Union as a result of enlargement. In the first place the Union and the countries themselves will face enormous challenges in conforming economically. Much has already been done and much has changed, especially in the former communist states. But there is still much to be done and there may be many problems in the coming years. The intention, however, is to bring the economic benefits of those already in the EU to these incoming nations. That, surely, is a worthy intention. Second, there is great anxiety, not least in this country, about the effects liberty of movement will bring. Some expect mass migration. I doubt that will happen, though some people may move from poorer to richer parts of the EU at least for a period of time until standards of living rise in the poorer regions. Measures are being taken in this and other older member countries to prevent abuses and these may have to be strengthened. Actually on the borders of the old EU many are anxious that the pressure may work in the opposite direction, with Germans looking for cheaper homes in western Poland or the Czech Republic for example. What is more, Britons and other citizens from the older EU nations are already buying up property in plum central European sites like Prague and Budapest. The third challenge, or rather opportunity, is cultural. And it is not yet fully with us. The countries acceding today are principally Catholic or Protestant. Their historic roots are tied to western rather than eastern Europe even if in the last sixty years they were in the so-called 'eastern block'. They are most appropriately called central European. There is plenty more of Europe to the east of Poland or Slovakia! However they do fringe onto what is genuinely eastern Europe where the culture was dominated by Orthodoxy. The absorption of this culture has already begun, of course, with the membership of Greece, but some of these countries, like Hungary, are bridges into that rather different cultural milieu.

The accession of ten new member states to the Union is a time of enlargement in every sense. The population of the EU enlarges to around 450 million, the economic community and free market is greatly enlarged, the opportunity for the interchange of peoples enlarges and the cultural sphere of the EU is enlarged. The question is, can we enlarge our vision to handle all this? It is an opportunity we must grasp and not neglect. And Christians should be at the forefront of this. They should be encouraging many forms of collective identity, local, regional, national, global. They should be involved in working together for peace, justice, democracy, human rights and prosperity throughout the European Union and beyond. They should be encouraging the newly enlarged EU to look to its wider responsibilities as well as its European ones. They could do well to follow the example of St Catherine of Siena, one of the three co-patronesses of Europe. In the confused politics of her day she saw it as her role to speak out boldly to those in authority, but also to act as a bridge-builder between competing factions. That is something we must do as individual Christians. And as institutions the churches of Europe can also play their part in enlarging the vision, providing opportunities for Christians and others across the continent to get to know and to trust each other. The enlargement of the European Union is a cause for hope. It is an opportunity we all should grasp to add a new layer to the multiple identity we enjoy in twenty first century Europe.

Notes

1. Quoted in P.H. Spaak, *The Continuing Battle: Memoirs of a European 1936-1966*, London, 1971, p. 212.
2. Origen, *Contra Celsum*, trans. H. Chadwick, Cambridge, 1965, II. 30 (p.92).
3. *Gaudium et Spes*, para. 75, in W.M. Abbott (ed.), The *Documents of Vatican II*, London: 1966, p. 286.
4. Ibid. para. 84, p. 298.
5. Wolfhart Pannenberg, *Ethics*, London, 1981, p.144.
6. The New Delhi Report: *The Third Assembly of the World Council of Churches 1961*, London, 1962, p.106.
7. Pannenberg, op.cit., pp. 147-148.
8. Oliver O'Donovan, *The Desire of the Nations*, Cambridge, 1996, p.268.
9. Keith Archer (ed.), *The Future of Europe*, Manchester, 1997, p.17.
10. Michael Howard, *The Lessons of History*, Oxford, 1991, p.39.
11. Zygmunt Bauman, *Modernity and Ambivalence*, Cambridge, 1991, p. 249.
12. Anthony D. Smith, *National Identity*, Harmondsworth, 1991, p. 174.
13. in Keith Archer, op. cit.
14. Mark Leonard, *Making Europe Popular, the Search for European Identity*, London, DEMOS, 1998, p.23.
15. Ibid.
16. Ibid. p.24.
17. See 'Building a Collective European Identity through the Media', *EIM Internet Bulletin*, 3/97.
18. Schuman Declaration, 1950, para. 2.
19. Treaty of Paris, 1950, preamble.
20. Andrew Goddard, *The European Union: A Christian Perspective*, Cambridge, 1998, pp.15-17.